Successful Budgeting For The Single Daddy

How To Budget For Single Dads Looking To Live A Balanced Life

Nick Thomas

Copyright © 2015 Nick Thomas

All rights reserved

No part of this book may be reproduced in any form or by any electronic or mechanical means including information storage and retrieval systems, without permission in writing from the author. The only exception is by a reviewer, who may quote short excepts in a review.

Although the author and publisher have made every effort to ensure that the information in this book was correct at press time, the author and publisher do not assume and hereby disclaim any liability to any party for any loss, damage, or disruption caused by errors or omissions, whether such errors or omissions result from negligence, accident, or any other cause.

Visit my website at www.singledaddydating.com

ISBN-13: 978-1505405538

ISBN-10: 150540553X

JOIN OUR COMMUNITY!

Single Daddy Dating is a growing community of single fathers who look to help each other, not only with dating success but in all areas of their lives too. This includes parenting, career and finances advice.

Join us today and get '**10 Crucial Checklist To Dating Success For Single Fathers**' completely FREE!

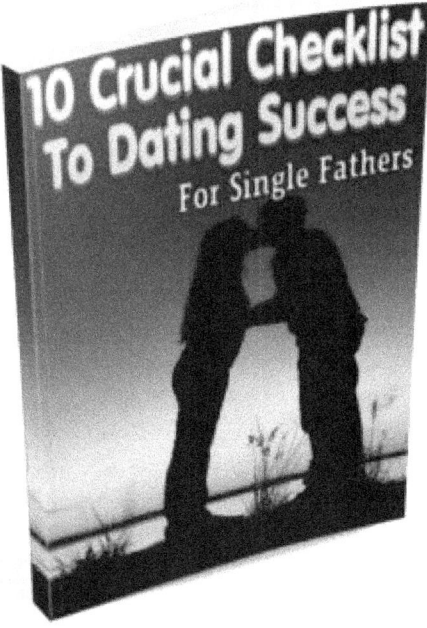

JOIN US AT
WWW.SINGLEDADDYDATING.COM/NEWSLETTER/

NICK THOMAS   www.singledaddydating.com

CONTENTS

Chapter 1: Financial Dilemma Of Single Fathers........... 1

Chapter 2: The Emotional Stress Of Budgeting 8

Chapter 3: Steps To Start Budgeting 16

Chapter 4: Best Budgeting Strategies Shared By Single Fathers 26

Chapter 5: Other Tips That Impact Your Finances 33

Chapter 6: Look To Make More Money....................... 39

Chapter 1: Financial Dilemma Of Single Fathers

Letter from Dave:

Nick,

I am divorced for three years as of this April. Things have been difficult ever since the divorce proceedings were finalized.

I still remember the day when the judge gave me sole custody over the children. I was over the moon.

I still needed to pay alimony but knowing that I have rights over my two children meant the world to me. My ex-wife wasn't a responsible person and the court knew that. She didn't stay at home to take care of the children while we were together. After the divorce, I needed to take a clean break.

Fast forward three years, and I realize that things haven't got easier. Although you teach a lot about dating, I was hoping you could share with me some ideas on how to manage my finances.

Over the past three years, I have been stressing a lot about my finances. From credit card debt to accruing on my utility payments, I always wake up feeling like someone is there to 'get' me.

I'm not interested in dating at all. I simply don't have the time or money for it.

My eldest daughter would be entering junior high soon. I hate the fact that I'm doing so badly financially. I feel so irresponsible for letting them down and not having good financial health.

Help! What should I do?

Dave, from Long Island.

***

Many single fathers tend to get into trouble with their money after a divorce. Even if they have 'escaped' alimony and child support, it can still be difficult for single fathers if they have custody of the child. This is because being a single father means that you have to deal with the situations alone.

You don't have a partner to help you in certain situations. Previously, you may have a partner who helps pick up the children when you are busy or helped you with the management of the finances. Now, things have changed. You are alone and filled with tons of responsibilities. Chiefly, parenting and making a living.

They also tend to spend emotionally after the divorce. The divorce may have impacted them to an extent that they find it hard to focus on their lives. They spend unnecessarily to try forget the pain of the past. I have known men who buy luxury cars or go on expensive holidays after divorce, in an attempt to get over their painful divorce.

They might also try to buy stuffs for their children to win over their hearts. Should they be in the middle of a tensed custody battle, they may buy their children stuffs to win over their hearts. Even if they don't have the money, they would buy them by signing it on their credit cards.

Over time, they stare at a huge mountain of debt with no way out. They have no idea how to manage the debt because they are so busy paying off the debt with the expenses piling up.

Not only do they need to pay for the 'big' expenses like the mortgage and alimony, they also need to care about the other 'smaller' expenses that can amount to a big figure when added up. These 'smaller' expenses might be food, children trips, gas for the car and many more.

Therein lies the importance of budgeting. Budgeting is important for the single father because they need to plan their spending. If you fail to plan your spending, you only get into more financial trouble. You may end up in debt or you won't have money for any 'future' plans such as your child's college or retirement.

Let me remind you about the costs of bringing up a child. According to a report by a US government agency, it would cost an estimated $240k for a middle-income couple to raise a child from the first day the child is born up till the child's 18th birthday. If that's difficult for a couple, it would be even more difficult for a single parent.

However, you don't need to feel so bad about being a single father. The one main positive point about being a single father is the fact that you won't have a partner to bicker with. You make ALL the financial decisions. You know where you want your money to be and how you intend to plan the future.

Your ex-wife may be the one who pays the bills and make those financial decisions in the past. If that's the case, then you need to start learning the way to do it. You need to take some time to learn about budgeting and saving money. Don't let numbers overwhelm you.

Not every single father is running on financial fumes and dwelling in self-pity. There are plenty of single father who are thriving and doing great. But, if you are a single father who sometimes find yourself staring at the bank account and wondering how to manage your finances, this book would be there to help you.

From this book, you would learn about the

basics of budgeting. It covers the basic steps on how to budget and help you deal with the emotional challenges of budgeting. Emotions play a big role in budgeting, as you would learn in the next chapter.

Chapter 2: The Emotional Stress Of Budgeting

If dealing with numbers come naturally to you, great. If not, budgeting can be a real nightmare. It was tough for me to understand at first because I was natural with it, but some people do have a terrible time with numbers.

For me, budgeting came naturally. I was always good with numbers. Ever since I was in school, I was good in math. I always scored well in any subjects that needed calculations.

But wait, budgeting isn't all about math.

In fact, budgeting is more about planning than math. Even if you are good in math, it doesn't mean that you can plan well. Of course, being good in math help, but it isn't the main factor to being a good budgeter. The essence of a good budgeter lies in having these few attributes:-

- **Planning.** Someone who budgets well is someone who plans well. He understands what he plans to do with his money. A person with good planning skills would be able to foresee where his money goes each month. From this, he would be able to set aside how much money he needs for certain expenses each month.

- **Prioritising.** A big part of planning is learning how to prioritise. What is important to you now? You would need to plan your finances around the spending which are important. For a single father, that might include food and paying off the mortgage.

- **Execution.** It isn't enough to only plan your budgeting. You also need to execute. Execution is tested when you seem tempted to buy some things. Probably it is a nice mobile phone you see in the supermarket or the brand new car. Execution is having the strength to stay within your budget when you seem tempted to spend otherwise.

- **Emotional Control.** As a single father, you would face certain situations that would test your emotional strength. Part of you feel like spending that sort of money because it fulfils a certain emotional need. Without having control over your emotions, it would be very easy for you to spend without caring about the future.

For many people, budgeting is very stressful because they have yet to do it before. The moment they start to budget, they realize that their money is limited. This makes them uncomfortable and stressed. My sister is someone like that.

From a young age, she wasn't known to be a budgeter. She would spend whatever money my parents gave her. It is to no one's surprise that she was heavily in debt by the time she reached 25 years old.

The moment she has to handle her 'numbers', she would get an anxiety attack. She simply had no confidence with dealing with numbers.

Being a single father, you may face some problems with your budgeting too. There are times where you realize your children would greatly increase your spending. Children cost a lot of money.

When they ask you to buy something, it takes a lot of emotional strength to say no. This is even more so when you have recently been divorced. There seem to be an attempt to deal with the emotional guilt by buying whatever they want.

Even if you say no to what they want, you would still be tested in other ways. They would have certain class trips which costs money. Some of those trips have been known to cost a fair deal. Do you allow them to participate?

This puts you in a dilemma. You find it hard to say no because you want to give the best to your children but at the same time, you are wondering if it is really that important. Don't feel bad, it is only natural for a father to want the very best for his children. At the same time, you are also being responsible for wanting to spend only what is needed.

These are some tips that single fathers have shared in managing their finances. Among the tips include:-

- **Portion your spending to daily**

amounts. When deciding on the amount of money as an expense each day. It would be better to proportion it to how much you can spend each day. This means that if you have a $300 budget for food each month, you would have a $10 budget each day. When you have such a 'target amount', you won't spend that much each day. It helps to know that you have $X amount each day rather than having $X each month, which would only make you overspend. – *Ross* –

- **Spend On Food Last.** It may seem counterintuitive, but it makes sense. "I would pay my bills first and buy food second. I wouldn't be able to spend what I don't have" Simon said. He says that budgets can be destroyed by having a poorly planned or impulsive grocery spending. If you spend on food first, you would tend to overspend. If you decide to pay for housing and bills first, then you would think that you have less money and not spend too much. – *Simon* –

- **Explain To Your Children.** When your children is old enough to understand (usually after 10 years old), you can share with them your financial problems. It is no shame really. It is part of life. Telling them about my problems make me closer to them. They even find for ways to make my life easier. My youngest son started to make his own lunch to bring to school. "You don't have to give me pocket money to buy food in school, Dad. I would just pack something from home." I felt proud. – *Joey* –

I am thankful for these single fathers who share with me their budgeting experience. These are just some tips that you would find from this book. I have known of many single fathers who have been able to manage their finances well, even if they are a single parent.

It is easier to keep on top of your finances than you think. It can be easy when you start to learn from other people. In the next chapter, I would share some step-by-step methods of budgeting.

Chapter 3: Steps To Start Budgeting

Even if you don't make much, it is still possible for you to live well. You can still save for retirement, have a college fund and make sure that your children eat well. All parents want to give their children the best. I'm sure it's the same for you, since you are reading this book.

When it comes to budgeting, it is important to know that you can get financial help. There are many agencies out there who would help single parents with their finances. As long you have children, you would be surprised by the number of agencies out there willing to help.

Simply contact your local social service agency. They would give you advice and guidance for food, medical attention, housing aid and even financial advice. Other organizations like charities or churches may offer extra help during the holiday period.

In this chapter, you learn about the various steps to start budgeting and having a better financial future.

Goals & Plans

If you feel that you wouldn't be able to support yourself and your children with the same finances, then you need to think of increasing your income. You need to look for ways to make more money. You would learn about this in Chapter 6 – Look To Make More Money.

There is only so much money you can save by reducing your expenses.

For now, you should look to set some financial goals. Determine a number that you want to save by one year and then divide it by the number of months. For example, if you want to save $6,000 by the end of one year, you would need to save $500 each month. This becomes your monthly savings target.

You also need to consider the expenses you need to incur each month. How much do you budget for your spending? Allocate a certain budget for your food, travel and emergency fund. Certain expenses such as utility bills, day care or educational costs should also be determined.

If one of your goals is to make more money, consider the cost of additional education. You can easily educate yourself by attending a local community college after work or an online education. This would be one of your goals.

As you have set your goals, write it down on a piece of paper (a journal would be better). Make sure to be as clear as possible about the goals that you have. Clarity would help you achieve your goals much faster.

Live According To Your Income

When it comes to budgeting, you need to work with what you have and avoid debt at all costs. If you are having debt each month, it means that you aren't budgeting well. It could also mean that you aren't living according to your income.

The following tips can help you live according to your income:-

- **Cheaper Housing.** There are always cheaper housing available or housing allowance given to ensure that you can survive as a single father. See if you are paying too much on your monthly rental and mortgage. It pays to do some research.

- **Limit Utility Use.** Try to reduce the usage of electricity and water if you find that the bills are too high. Tell your children about the need to save some money.

- **Strategic Travelling.** Only travel when you are sending your children to school and going to work. Do errands like grocery shopping or paying for utilities on the way. This would save a great deal on gas.

- **Find Cheaper Transportation.** If possible, use the public transport. You can sell the car if you are paying too much in car loan or maintenance expenses. You can choose to take a bus, train or even walk, if feasible.

Grocery Expenses

Grocery expenses would take up a huge deal of your budget. Besides housing and alimony, this may easily be the next highest expense in your budget. It can be hard to save by cutting down on the food you buy. These are some tips that single fathers can use to reduce grocery expenses:-

- **Use Coupons.** Cut out coupons from newspapers or magazines. Use them well, and you would be able to save a great deal. I have known some people who are able to buy groceries of up to $300 and pay only pennies. Check out this link to know more about Power Couponing

  www.singledaddydating.com/couponing

- **Use Customer Reward Cards.** If you always frequent a store, look to be their loyal customer by joining their reward cards. You would be able to save quite a bit of money.

- **Learn To Cook.** If you learn how to cook economically, you would save more money on food. In fact, you can look to cook in bulk so you don't have to waste so much electricity on cooking.

- **Buy In Bulk.** Whenever shopping for groceries, see if you can buy in bulk. This gives you a cheaper rate. However, you need to be careful as to not buy perishable items that can't last long. It would only be a waste of money if it expires.

- **Join Mailing Lists.** Some supermarkets or shopping malls have mailing list where the send coupons, samples and rebates. Join as many mailing list to get the first hand news on certain savings you can make.

Different single fathers have their own ways of saving on expenses. One great way is to join single parent support groups. Some of these support groups have bulk purchase groups where they buy some groceries in bulk. Because of this, their groceries can be pretty cheap.

Ask around the members of the support group if there is such a thing. If there isn't, you can even start one. Ask around to see if anyone is keen on such bulk purchase. If they are, you can slowly source from supermarkets. Tell the supermarket manager that you have a group of buyers who are willing to purchase in bulk.

Don't Buy Unnecessary Possessions

The things you own ends up owning you. By having too many possessions, you would find it hard to save towards your financial goals. Try to keep your life as simple as possible. Simplicity allows you to get ahead in life.

Limit the amount of clothing you have. Do you actually use most of the clothing you have? Why not give away some of your clothing and stop buying clothing for a while?

When you really need to buy clothes, visit thrift stores or consignment shops to get them. You can also find toys and household items at yard sales.

Simply put, you can live with less. Much less. Look around at the things you own and see if you can sell them. Most of the things you have, you don't even need. Why waste time keeping them?

***

When it comes to budgeting, the most essential is to have a long term view about where you are using your money. If you truly find it difficult to do so, you can ask someone else for help. Never be too proud to ask for help. You can ask single fathers in a single father support group for help too.

You need to change a lot of things in your life as you realize the financial goals that you have. You may need to change some of the bad spending habits and activities that you have. These may be difficult at first, but give it some time. It would be worth it when you see yourself saving more money for your own financial future.

Chapter 4: Best Budgeting Strategies Shared By Single Fathers

If you don't keep tabs on your spending, you would end up in debt. In our current economy, it seems so easy to get into debt due to the ease of credit. That is where budgeting becomes so important. It becomes even more important when your income is tight.

In this chapter, I would share some strategies share from single fathers whom have sent in their advice. Many of them are single fathers I met at support group meetings. Some of them have become close confidants. These tips are short but it can be very helpful when executed.

Justin

One important thing I do is to always check my bank statement and credit card statement to check for my expenses. Cutting out luxuries and highlighting certain items that has cost too much would help me budget better. I make a mental note to cut down on a certain expense and stop buying those luxuries in the next month.

Nicholas

Always check if you have certain entitlements. There are plenty of benefits to make your life easier. Why struggle when you can have the government help you? I have used them to great effect. It has helped me saved hundreds each month.

Sillaci

Check for monthly payments on your gas, electricity, internet and insurance. Most countries have websites where you can compare the prices. Choose one which has the most value based on what you need. The cheapest doesn't mean the best for you. Think about what you need. Do the hard work and you can save some money.

Ledley

Research your shopping. Different places would have sales. Think of ways to make food shopping and other purchases cheaper. As a single father, you need to have a place where you constantly buy your items. See if there's a loyalty programs where you can get some points.

Wayne

I realized that I was paying too much on my mortgage three years back. I got a broker to help me get the best deal. He got me a fantastic deal!

Although I would need to pay him some money (commission), the savings has given me great returns. Pay a broker to get you good mortgage rates. You may not realize that you have been paying too high an interest.

Chris

Fun things don't need to cost too much money. Our single father support group has many budget-conscious members. We would have a potluck every month to meet up and for the children to have fun.

Each one only needs to cook for two people.

If you come with two children, you only need to cook for three. We have great 'budget-conscious' fun. My children look forward to it each month.

Mitchell

Budgeting tools can be very helpful. I have used them to manage my expenses. If you are finding it difficult to find the proper tool, simply use Microsoft Excel. There are iPhone or Android apps out there that can help you budget effortlessly.

Mitch

Save first, spend later. This is my mantra. If I don't pay myself first, who would? I save a minimum of 20% of my monthly income the moment I get it. It becomes a habit. The excess is used to pay my bills and buy food. I also save the extras into my children's college fund.

Edwin

Have a vision for your finances. Most people find it hard to save and budget for a simple reason – they have no purpose for their money. They don't have a 'dream' for their money.

You need to dream big if you want to have the motivation to save more money. My motivation to save comes from the fact that I want to retire by the age of 45. I am 37 this year. I have saved over $300k and am looking to invest in properties so I can retire early. My children think that I am a cheap miser, but I see myself as a motivated single father looking to provide for my children's future.

Irvin

Automation is the key to saving consistently. I save at least 30% of my monthly income. I make it automated. My salary comes in at the

1st of each month. I am paid $8,000 each month. On the 2nd of each month, there's a standing order on my bank account to transfer $3,000 to my other bank account.

I automate it. As such, I only 'make' $5,000 each month. Knowing this, I make sure that I limit my expenses. I have never touched the money from the other account. Last I checked, I have saved around $112,000.

Chapter 5: Other Tips That Impact Your Finances

Raising children and finances – two of the most difficult tasks in the world. According to experts, single parents should have a balanced strategy that meets the emotional and financial needs of their family.

On average, raising a child until he or she reaches 18 is $240,000. You need to be in tip top financial condition to ensure you have peace of mind with your financial matters.

In this chapter, you would learn about other

factors that play an important role in your financial health.

- **Have Clear Priorities.** Be clear about what's important to you. You can't expect to have everything in life. When spending money, think of what's most important for the family. Is the vacation more important than fixing the water heater? Priorities are important when it comes to spending.

- **Prepare Your Estate.** You may not like to hear it, but shit happens. Make sure that you have a will in place and a guardian named to take care of your children should something happens to you. Ideally, you should even have a financial plan for your child's future. Besides that, having a life insurance policy is very important for a single father.

- **Be Clear About Your Security Level.** How much uncertainty can you handle in life? When you are first starting to save for your child's college fund and he is still young, you may go for higher-risk investment. Once he is about to enter college, make sure that you switch to a lower risk one. Understanding different stages of your life helps to understand whether you should take more or less risks.

- **Income Tax Deductions.** Child care deductions would lower your taxes paid. If you are a single father, you would get a favourable income tax rate for filing single. Always be up to date with the latest changes in the income tax rules. It would save you a lot of money. Ignorance is bliss, but it can also cost you.

- **You Own Your Own Job Security.** If you are employed, do a good job. If you are the great employee in your company, you have great job security. The qualities you can do to ensure your job security is to have impeccable ethics, good work habits and volunteer for any company activities that you can. Such a mindset ensures that you won't be the one that is retrenched if something happens.

- **Teach Children Money.** Your children play a big role in your daily expenses. You would be surprised by how much they can help you save if you share with them your problems. Talking to them about money can be tough, but it is something they would need to learn sooner or later. It is part of life. Having them deal with the 'real' part of life at a younger age would definitely be better for them.

- **Child Support.** Most of the time, a single father would need to pay for child support. However, there are times where the mother would pay the father child support. This is in situations where the court judged that the father is a better guardian than the mother after a divorce. If so, you need to keep an eye on your ex-wife's earnings. If she has an increase in earnings, you have an opportunity to petition to the court for an increase in financial support.

- **Take Care Of Yourself.** Nothing means anything if you don't have good health. As a single father, you would need to give yourself a break once in a while. Doing this would make you a much better provider and caretaker. There are way too many parents who are stressed up that their children are afraid to be around them. Find time to do things that you enjoy. Do some exercises if you need to. Meet some friends. Doing things that you enjoy gives you the motivation to do greater things as a parent and a provider.

Many of these tips are simply common advice given to ensure your well-being. Having a good well-being would impact your finances tremendously. When dealing with your finances, it pays to have good emotional health. Those who tend to have better emotional or mental health tend to do better financially.

Chapter 6: Look To Make More Money

From the very first chapter, I have shared about the importance of budgeting. In fact, this entire book is about budgeting, if you have forgotten the title.

However, budgeting only isn't enough. It is also important to look for avenues to make more money. You have to be looking for ways to make more money in your life. You can't expect to cut out all the expenses in your life. There is always a limit to how much money you save, but there's no limit to how much money you can make.

Do you have the intentions of making more money?

Even if you have a job that requires you to put in long hours and having to put in long hours as a single father, it is still possible for you to make more money. There are many businesses you can start online and help relieve the financial burden that you face.

When starting to make more money, you should keep in mind the following:-

- **Start With Time Management.** Time is the one thing that prevents most of us from making more money. As a single father, time seems to be so precious. We struggle to even have a few minutes for ourselves. Making more money seems difficult because of it. As such, always look to manage your time well. Learn time management methods from books. Time management is perhaps the one skills that makes life as a single father manageable.

- **Downsize First.** When it comes to making more money, you would need to downsize first. Try to live a minimalist life where you focus on the bare essentials in life. You can't expect to get ahead and make more money when your life is riddled with unnecessary debt – buying things you don't need and paying a high interest rate on it.

- **Have A Long Term View.** Always know where your money is heading. *What do you intend to do in the future? When do you plan to retire? Are you planning to save for your children's college fund?* All these are factors that play into your considerations while budgeting. Besides that, they also become a motivating factor in your decision to make money. Reflect on your long term view from time to time to get better clarity.

- **Set Priorities.** Know your priorities in life. As a single father, you should look to be a parent that is there for his children. You must also think of your future. Don't spend too much time on unnecessary pursuits like activities that simply waste time or going out with friends who aren't helping you in life. You want to set aside time for activities that make your life better. Instead of spending time on those wasteful activities like drinking or playing poker, go learn a new skill instead that can help you with your job or makes you more money.

- **Reduce And Eliminate Debt.** Debt binds you. As simple as that. If you want to make more money, you must look to eliminate debt first. If you have a pile of debt that you must pay each month, it would be hard for you to get ahead.

Once you have a simple life where you don't have any debt, you are in a great position to build your income. Remember, the higher your income, the more freedom you have. However, don't increase your expenses to an extent that it doesn't make any difference at all. Many people, once they make more money, tend to spend even more. Their expenses rise together with their income. They never get ahead then.

I love simplicity because it allows me to try new things. When you have low expenses, you are able to try a myriad of things without worrying too much. It is because of such simple lifestyle that allows me to live the life I am living and have a business of my own.

If you want to fly very far, you need to carry very little.

LEAVE A REVIEW

I hope this book has helped you well. It isn't my intention at all to go deep into the topic. I am no expert in everything. However, I have the help of many other single fathers who have shared with me their invaluable experience.

If this book has helped you in any way, do leave me a review. This helps build our single father community.

If you feel that this book can be improved in any way, do mention it in the review. I would love to hear from you.

I wish you luck as a single father…

ABOUT NICK THOMAS

Nicholas Thomas has helped many single fathers cope with divorce in the past few years. By helping them gain more confidence and stability in their lives, he is able to guide them towards being a man that attracts other women easily.

He divorced back in 2008 and knows how difficult a divorce can be for a man. It was a terrible time for him when he got his divorce. He envisioned his children blaming him and not being able to spend time with him. It gave him a constant guilt trip.

Being a divorced man can be very difficult. Ever since his 'emotional recovery' from the divorce, he has helped many single fathers by advising and helping them gain confidence.

Should you want to share your story with him, you can do so at
www.singledaddydating.com/shareastory/

ALSO BY NICK THOMAS

(1) Dating After Divorce For The Single Daddy

(2) Dating Ideas For The Single Daddy

(3) How To Be An Alpha Male

(4) First Date Conversations

(5) Online Dating

(6) How To Approach Women

(7) Mature Dating

(8) Single Parent Support

(9) Coping With Divorce

(10) Parenting After Divorce

Visit www.singledaddydating.com/bookstore/

Get Your Complimentary
FREE BOOK

Join our community today and get **10 Crucial Checklist To Dating Success For Single Fathers** FREE, delivered right to your email…

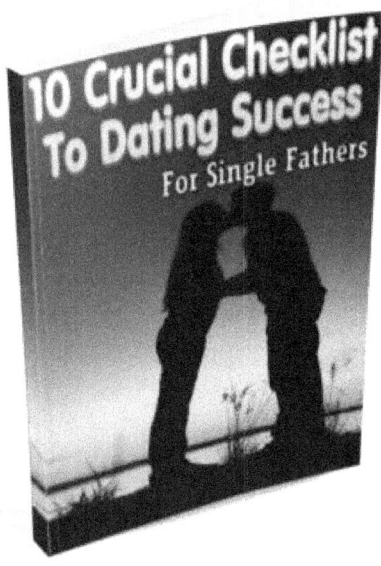

JOIN US AT
WWW.SINGLEDADDYDATING.COM/
NEWSLETTER/

www.ingramcontent.com/pod-product-compliance
Lightning Source LLC
Chambersburg PA
CBHW071823170526
45167CB00003B/1397